Hot Air Balloons

Written by
Cath Jones

Ransom

I am Sheep.
This is Rooster,
and that is
Duck.

Back in 1783 we went up
in a hot air balloon. It was fantastic!

They said we were test travellers.
In the winter of that year,
they sent some men up too.

But **we** started it!

2

The men went up in the winter of 1783 in this balloon.

3

A hot air balloon
is like an aircraft,
but it is lighter than air!

It has a big, fabric air bag containing hot
air, with a little vent at the top.

The balloons have containers for travellers,
hanging down under the air bag.

A burner under the air bag aims
hot air into the balloon.

To get the balloon to hover at the right
speed, you must keep turning the burner
on and off.

When the burner is off, the air cools
and the balloon starts to go down.

When the burner is back on, the air gets
hotter and the balloon starts to go up.

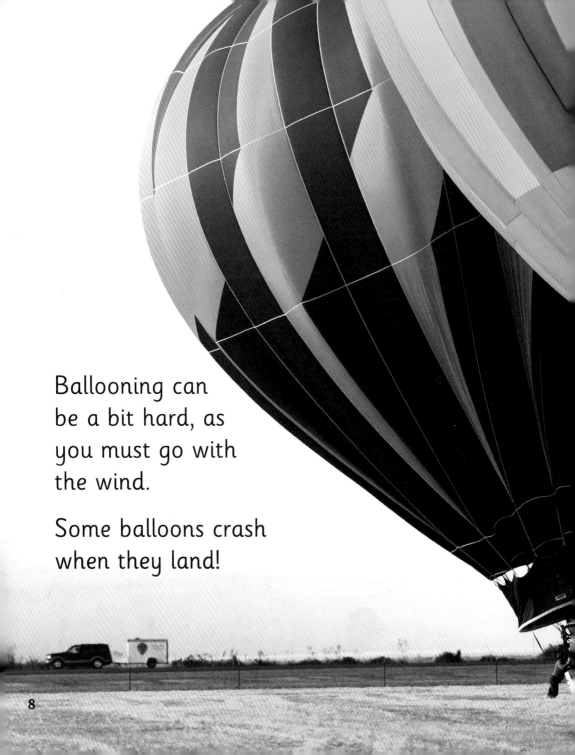

Ballooning can
be a bit hard, as
you must go with
the wind.

Some balloons crash
when they land!

At a balloon fair,
lots of balloons are
in the air together.

This is when you get to see
lots of fantastic balloons.

Can you see a boot?

You do not need to go to an airport to go up in a balloon.

Just get the balloon out of the van or the truck, get some hot air and up you go!

What fun!

Travellers like to go on balloon trips
to see things from up high.

What do you think the travellers
in this balloon are looking for?

In 1991, a balloon went up higher than Everest.

In 1783, Duck, Rooster and I went just as high as a big tower.

WOW!

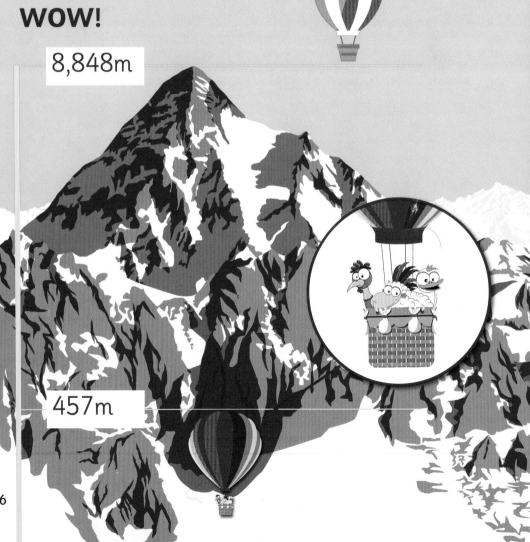

8,848m

457m